D1728073

PASTOR WADE'S LESSONS OF THE WORD

PASTOR WADE'S LESSONS OF THE WORD

MELVIN V. WADE, SR.

Urban Publishing House, LLC

Foreword

As a student at Bishop College, I asked the Dean of the Chapel, Dr. Harry S. Wright, a masterful illustrator who always provided the student audience with an attention arresting oratorical video of vivid images, captivating stories, and moving metaphors in his chapel sermons, what was the key to finding illustrations? He replied, "I view life through homiletical eyeglasses." He went on to explain that he had learned from our Savior, the Supreme Storyteller, who lifted lessons from the everyday lives of everyday people to portray the Reign and Rule of God. The inspiring insights of Jesus were taken from the experiences His audience could identify with. His listeners were aware of the dangers of the Jericho Road and immediately could feel the emotions, experiences, and fear of the participants in the parable of the Samaritan who risked so much to do good. The crowd had heard or personally experienced the heartbreak of a child leaving home and engaging in rebellious prodigality. The homiletical eyeglasses of Jesus were at work in the Sermon on the Mount as He encouraged those afflicted with anxiety to "behold the birds of the air" and look at the "lilies of the field" because God provides for the birds, and even the splendor of Solomon couldn't match the "fly fashions" of the wildflowers. Jesus Christ evidently wore homiletical eyeglasses and brilliantly used illustrations and imagery to reveal who God is and what it means to be a Christ-follower.

The Reverend Doctor Melvin Von Wade, Sr., is a faithful follower of Jesus, and for many years, he has been admired and applauded, copied, and celebrated for his preaching prowess and sermonic artistry. He meticulously crafts sermons that are biblically based, prayer saturated,

Christ-centered, and remarkably relevant. He has always been able to reach multiple generations. To use the vernacular of the culture, "Wade is a beast" in the pulpit! One of the reasons that he is so powerful in the pulpit is that he can build an argument like a lawyer and illustrate his ideas out of the 20/20 vision of his "homiletical eyeglasses." Like Jesus, he can capture one's attention with a well-placed story that he narrates with the benefit of a wealthy vocabulary that allows the congregation to "see" what he is saying. His illustrations are windows that allow the witness to view the Word and connect that Word so that it lives in and through the witnessing worshipper. To use the language of the late Rev. Manuel L. Scott, Sr., Wade's preaching is "portable; one can package the message, and carry it home" because his illustrations are moving and memorable.

Dr. Wade has gifted us with this book of illustrations. Preachers and public speakers will gratefully use this as an inspiring resource for their sermons and speeches. Some will be blessed to read devotionally these uplifting anecdotes. Even children and young people would be advised to read and be edified by the sagacious lessons that leap from the pages. Some readers will even feel like the saints of old when they heard preachers using illustrations and narrating biblical stories with poetic flair, and like them, you may want to respond, "Paint the picture," or "tell the story," or "Don't ya see!" All will thank God for the imagination and homiletical eyeglasses that Melvin Von Wade, Sr. so faithfully wears.

Frederick Douglass Haynes III
Senior Pastor, Friendship-West Baptist Church
Dallas, Texas

First Printing, 2022

First published by Urban Publishing House, LLC 2022

P.O. Box 1684
Oxnard, CA 93032
805.609.4951
urbanpublishinghouse.com

Contents

Introduction

In all honesty, at the beginning of my ministry, I was not into sermon illustrations. I was introduced to the idea of sermon Illustrations by one of my homiletics professors at Perkins Theological Seminary in Dallas, Texas. However, I did not really grasp the idea of sermon illustrations. While in Dallas, I purchased some sermon illustration books, but they did not seem to register with me.

Prov. 27:17 reads, "Iron sharpeneth iron, so a man sharpeneth the countenance of his friend." I referred to this passage because that is exactly what happened to me as it relates to sermon illustrations. I had some friends who impacted me with the idea of sermon illustrations. There were three in particular. They were: (1) E. K. Bailey, (2) Freddie Haynes, and (3) Norman Owens. The first thing they faced me with was the fact that the greatest illustrator was Jesus. That's what the parables were about.

Then, I was introduced to the idea of illustrations from personal life experiences. And then, life's experiences from the personal experiences of others impacted my use of sermon illustrations. So, I owe these three individuals who opened my eyes to the significance and the relevance of sermon illustrations, plus my professor at Perkins, a great deal of thanks.

There will be many who did not hear many of the great preachers of the 20th century. In this book, there are illustrations that come from some of them. As far as a number of the illustrations are concerned, I don't remember who I heard them from. I remember hearing some of them before I started preaching.

So, I hope that this compilation of illustrations will be most relevant and helpful to you, and if you are not into illustrations, I hope that following the example of Jesus, as He used parables and illustrations, what you find in this book will invite you to take a look at the importance of sermon illustrations.

I

God Will Incline

In December of 1986, my father James Commodore Wade, Sr. was stricken with a heart attack in Los Angeles, California. While the doctor was performing bypass surgery, my father had a stroke on the operating table. Because of that, **that took some of my strength to pray.**

While Daddy was in Brotman Medical Center, my wife's mother who was visiting with us, took sick, and we had to place her in the same hospital as our father. **That took some more of my strength to pray.**

My brother, James Commodore Wade, Jr., came to help and to see about our father. Our father acknowledged that he was dealing with a heart issue called, "Angina." **That took some more of my strength to pray.**

While dealing with these devastating illnesses that lessened my strength to pray, some members of our church at Mt. Moriah Baptist Church in Los Angeles led a coup, a mass uprising to oust me. They printed a book called, "*The Red Book*." Twice, they had my name on the front page of the African American newspaper for racketeering. **That took some more of my strength to pray.**

While dealing with the assaults and the attempts to oust me, I was carried to court twice; plus, I had to endure an all-day deposition. **That took some more of my strength to pray.**

In the midst of all these horrifying experiences, my teenage daughter Susaun took mysteriously ill, and we had to place her in the same hospital. **That took some more of my strength to pray.**

> *-With all of this on me, I was literally depleted of the strength to pray. But thank God that I have a God who "inclines"; and "incline" means, "to lean forward and bow down to catch a sound that is too faint to otherwise be heard."*

2

Lack of Spiritual Maturity

The story is that a boy fell out of bed one night. The next morning, while he was eating his breakfast, his mother asked him how he fell out of bed on that last night. He responded to his mother by saying, "Momma, I fell out of bed last night because I stayed too close to where I first got in."

And that's the lot of some Christians. They have not matured in the Faith because they have remained too close to where they first got in.

> *-That's why they have snorkeling shallow-water attire, rather than scuba diving, and deep-water equipment.*

3

⚜

You Don't Ever Know What
God Is Going To Do

A grandmother used to read Bible stories to her granddaughter every night. One night, the grandmother decided to see how those Bible stories were being received by her granddaughter. The grandmother said, "Baby do you like these little Bible stories that Grandmama be' reading to you at night?" Elatedly, the granddaughter said, "Yes, Grandmama, I love those Bible stories." Because of her elatedness, the grandmother said, "Baby, why do you like those Bible stories that Grandmama be' reading?" The little girl said, "Grandmama, I love those Bible stories because you don't ever know what God is going to do."

-That's why Christians should never miss worship because you don't ever know what God is going to do.

4

God's Lovingkindness

The late Dr. J. Vernon McGee, the radio preacher who hosted the "Through the Bible" radio program, said that a little girl was in Sunday School one Sunday. And while in class, the teacher asked, "Who knows the difference between kindness and lovingkindness?"

The little girl raised her hand, and said, "I know." And the teacher said, "Tell me the difference between kindness and lovingkindness."

The little girl said, "Kindness is when you ask your mother for some toast, and she gives you some toast. **Lovingkindness is when you ask your mother for some toast, and she gives you some toast with some jelly on it.**"

That's what Jerry Bridges calls, "God's uncalled for generosity."

> *-I had a deacon named Feniez Graham. With broken English, he prayed, "Lord, I thank you for my needs and my don't need."*

5

God's Internal Comfort

In 1966, my church by stewardship, Bethlehem Baptist Church in Dallas, Texas, gave me the money to buy a beautiful 1967 blue Plymouth Sport Fury. On the dashboard, it read, "AC and Heat."

In the year 1986, while pastoring Mt Moriah Baptist Church in Los Angeles, California, I bought a black 1986 Vanden Plas Jaguar. On the dashboard, it did not read, "AC and Heat." Instead, it read, **"Climate Control."**

I found out that the design of climate control was to give you a comfort zone on the inside, no matter what the weather was on the outside.

> *-God, being "The God of All Comfort" will give you internal comfort even though things externally are cataclysmic and catastrophic.*

6

*

Sin Is Lethal

The encyclopedia describes a carnivorous plant found in Australia called, "The Drosera" or the "Sundew" plant. On the tentacles are the special hairs called, "trichrome," which is a gluey goo called, "mucilage." When insects light on the gluey goo and indulge in it, the tentacles enfold and digest the insect. **What the insect has done is indulge itself to death.**

-*This is what lethal sin will do. I like how Dr. Gary L. Baugh puts it. He says, "Sin contaminates and deceives the mind, defiles the lips, blinds the eyes, shackles the feet, burdens the shoulders, weakens strength, defiles hands, pollutes desires, lowers morals, hardens conscience, paralyzes wills, "uncontrols" appetites, wounds spirits, poisons affection, corrupts imagination, damages character, weakens faith, spoils beauty, shames faces, shatters nerves, kills love, sickens the stomach, tarnishes testimonies, insults the intelligence, scars souls, and removes joy."*

7

Jesus Takes Our Place

When I was a boy, on Monday thru Friday at 4:00 p.m., "The Adventures of Superman" was on television. "Faster than a speeding bullet. More powerful than a locomotive; bending steel with his bare hands, and able to leap tall buildings in a single bound" were the words spoken as the show began.

I recall an episode when a man was in the electric chair. Just as the warden was pulling the lever down, Superman crashed through the walls and stuck his arms in the way. **All that was to go into the man went into the arms of Superman.**

-As I thought about it: When justice consigned man to eternal damnation; when justice was about to pull the lever on man, Jesus crashed through the walls of history, and on Calvary, He stuck His arms in the way, and all that should have gone into man went into the arms of Jesus.

8

A Liberating Storm

In Dallas, Texas, a woman was abducted by two men at the North Park Shopping Center, wrapped in duct tape, a blanket, and stuffed in the car trunk. She believed the men's intent was to rape, rob, and kill her. Getting to the outskirts of Dallas, for some reason, they took her out of the trunk and dumped her in a ditch. There, she began to murmur and complain, "Lord, I am your servant. I served you faithfully for many years. How could you let me die in a ditch all by myself?" Complaining, she hears thunder and lightning, then feels pouring rain and begins to murmur, "Lord I'm your child, and now, you are going to let me die in a ditch all by myself **in a storm**? Then, the rainwater got between her body and duct tape. She was able to wiggle her way free. When she got home, she told her family, **"God sent a storm in order to set me free."**

-There are some favorite sins and pet iniquities that have us bound and tied. As the old blues song said, "I'm into something that I can't shake-a- loose." So, since we can't untie ourselves from them, and since there is no such thing as self-liberation, God sends a liberating storm our way.

9

Trust God Alone

For many years, our mother, Mary Frazier Wade would tell us that she did not trust anybody but her and Jesus.

One day, I called home, and she said, "Melvin I have updated information." She said, "All of your lives, I told you all that I did not trust anybody but me and Jesus. She said, **"The update is that the other day, I did something so stupid until I have cut me out. Now, I don't trust nobody but Jesus."**

When we look at the Bible "One Anothers," it says, "Love one another, forgive one another, pray one for another, be at peace with each other, be devoted to one another, honor one another, instruct one another, live in harmony with one another, greet one another, kiss one another, serve one another, be kind and compassionate to one another, submit to one another, admonish one another, do not slander one another, pray one for another, and offer hospitality to one another."

Of all the "One Another's," we do not find where it says, "Trust one another." Everywhere we find trust in the Bible, it is always directed towards God.

"They that trust in the Lord shall be as Mount Zion, which cannot be removed, but abideth forever." - Psalm 125:1

"In thee, O Lord, do I put my trust." - Psalm 31:1

"Trust in the Lord with all thine heart, and lean not to thine own understanding." - Proverbs 3:5

"They that know thy name will put their trust in Thee." - Psalm 9:16

-And scholars say that Psalm 118:8 is the middle verse of the Bible. It reads, "It is better to trust in the Lord than to put confidence in man."

10

What God Does with Forgiven Sins

A young theology student and an old lady who knew God well would talk all of the time. Every time that they would meet, the old lady would tell the young theology student, "I talks' to God, and God talks to me!"

One day, as they were talking, the young student said, "Mother, you still talks' to God, and God talks to you?" She says, "Yes baby, I talks' to God, and God talks to me." He said to the mother, "The next time that you talks' to God, and God talks to you, ask Him what my last sin was. If God tells you what my last sin was, then I'll know that you talks' to God, and God talks to you."

As per usual, they met up again, and the young man *started on* the old lady. He said, "Mother, you still talks' to God, and God talks' to you?" She said, "Yes, I talks' to God, and God talks' to me." He said, "Do you remember what you were to ask God?" She said, "Yes, I was to ask God what your last sin was." He said, "Did you ask him?"

She said, "Yes, I asked Him." He said, "What did God say?" She said, **"God said, 'Because you confessed it, I forgot it.'"**

That's what happens when we, God's children, ask in a spirit of repentance for God to forgive us. As my late friend E. K. Bailey used to say, "God puts forgiven sins in His Divine Forgettery and has holy amnesia with them."

It is interesting that the Jordan River flows into the Dead Sea, which represents God casting our sins into the Sea of Forgetfulness. The Bible affirms this, for the Bible says that God:

1. Forgives them. - 1 John 1:9
2. Cleanses us from them. - Psalm 51 2
3. Purges us from them. - Psalm 51:7
4. Blots them out. - Psalm 51:9
5. Casts them behind His back. - Isaiah 38:17
6. Will cast them into the depths of the Sea. - Micah 7:19
7. Remembers them no more. - Isaiah 43:25, Hebrews 8:12
8. Covers them up. - Psalm 32:1
9. Removes them as far as the East is from the West. - Psalm 103:12
10. Forgets them. - Jeremiah 31:34

> -God is Holy and Righteous. As a result, God does not ignore our sins, but because of the death of Jesus, God placed Himself in a paradoxical position whereby He can hate sin, and yet, forgive and forget the sins of the repentant.

11

God Is in the Rear

A man took a shortcut to church one night by walking down an alley. While walking through the dark alley that night, all of a sudden, a man jumped out and asked the man for a light. The man reached in his pocket, got a match, lit the cigarette, and hurriedly moved on. The next morning, while he was drinking his coffee, as per usual, he sees this man's picture on the front page for murder. The man said to his wife, "Honey, I saw this man in the alley last night. He seemed like such a nice man. And now, he is arrested for murder." He said, "Honey, I'm going to go to the jail and see what happened to this man after I saw him." The churchman was allowed to speak to the man. He asked the man how he could've done such a thing, seeing that he seemed to be such a nice man. The man said to the churchman, **"I really intended to kill you, but when you lit my cigarette, I saw two men over your shoulders. That's why I didn't kill you."**

> *-Psalm 23.6 says, "Surely goodness and mercy shall follow me all the days of my life." Goodness and mercy are twin attributes of God. So, goodness and mercy are our rearguards.*

12

Faithful to the End

When I was a student at Bishop College in Dallas, Texas, my Church History professor was Dean Seals. While in that class, I was impacted by the story of Bishop Polycarp:

Bishop Polycarp was one of the three chief Apostolic Fathers. He was the second-century Bishop of Smyrna. Polycarp was appointed by the Apostle John to be Bishop of Smyrna. After having been brought to Faith by John, Polycarp was a noted teacher. Because he was an avowed Christian, citizens of Smyrna wanted him to disavow Christ or be killed. After having had several successful attempts to hide from the governor, Polycarp was found. Polycarp was bound and taken to the governor. The Proconsul was unsuccessful at having Bishop Polycarp deny Jesus. The result was that he was bound in chains, and under the weight of chains, he uttered these immortal words: **"For eighty and six years have I served Him, and He has never done me injury. How then can I now blaspheme my King and Savior?"** After warning the governor of the Eternal Fire, Polycarp was tied to the stake. After being tied to the stake, the fire was lit. However, the flames of the fire encircled Polycarp, but miraculously, the flames avoided him. But finally, a soldier executed Polycarp with a sword.

-Faithfulness is an "in spite of" virtue. Too many are faithful "because of" or "as long as." But we are called to be faithful no matter what. Revelation 2:10 says, "Be thou faithful unto death."

13

Strength from the Bible

One day, I had a mild cold. So, seeking to get rid of it, I went to a health food store in our area called, "Simply Wholesome." I went looking for some tea that was designed to get rid of this mild cold.

On February 17, 1999, I received a bone-marrow transplant that was the cure for me having Leukemia. After that transplant, my wife, Jacquie, told me to "always read the fine print." So, following her instructions, I picked up a box of tea that was designed for colds. When I read the fine print, the fine print began preaching to me. That fine print said, **"The longer you soak it, the stronger it gets."**

-And that's what happens when we soak our souls in the Word of God. Jesus said in John 15:7, "If ye abide in me, and my words abide in you, you shall ask what you will, and it shall be done unto you." Psalm 119:28b says, "Strengthen thou me according to thy Word."

14

Familiarity and Closeness Seem to Dwarf Greatness

A man was said to have gone from Alabama to New York to see the Empire State Building, which was his heart's desire. When he arrived in New York, he made his way to Manhattan, seeking to find the Empire State Building. The man searched, but his search was in vain. Finally, after futilely searching, he stopped a passer-by and asked him if he knew where the Empire State Building was. The man responded by saying, **"You are standing in front of it."**

The man was standing in the presence of monumental greatness and couldn't see it because he was too close.

> *-How often are we guilty of the fact that we can't see greatness in some people because we are just too close? Nearness and closeness seem to dwarf greatness.*

15

All God Does Is Win

My granddaughter Sydné and I went to a basketball game one day. The home team won the basketball game. After the home team won, there was this loud music playing. I asked my granddaughter, "Syd, who was that?" She said that it was "DJ Khaled." I said, "What is he saying?" She said, "Poppi, he is saying, **"All I do is win."** As I pondered that thought, I said, "That's God's theme song." When we really look at it, all God does is win. Even when it looks like God is not winning, He is still winning. When the Satanic got Jesus on the Cross, it looks like Jesus is not winning. But according to 1Peter 3:19, between Friday and Sunday, He went and "preached unto the spirits in prison." The late Dr. Sandy F. Ray, former pastor of the Cornerstone Baptist Church in Brooklyn, New York expounded this verse. With vivid theological imagination, he said, "Jesus slipped away into Hell and rode His chariot through Hell, wrapping His chariot wheels around, death, Hell, and the grave. And the hosts of Hell said, 'ride on conquering King.'"

> *-The ultimate proof that God always wins is that "early Sunday morning, Jesus got up from the grave, with all power in His hands!"*

16

Is God Real?

An atheist doctor once asked an old preacher if God is real. The old preacher answered with an emphatic, "Yes!" The atheist doctor then asked the preacher a series of questions. The atheist asked the old preacher, "Have you ever seen God?" The preacher said, "No." He asked, "Have you ever heard God?" The old preacher said, "No." He asked, "Have you ever touched God?" The preacher said, "No." The doctor asked, "Have you smelled God?" The old preacher said, "No." Finally, he asked, "Have you ever tasted God?" The old preacher said, "No." The doctor said, "That ought to tell you that God is not real."

Elatedly, the doctor walked away, feeling like he had won the victory. What the doctor didn't know was that God is a "Right Now, Revelational God." He is quicker than right now, and sooner than at once, God gave that old preacher instant revelation.

As a result of God's immediate revelation, the old preacher called the doctor back. The old preacher asked the doctor a question. He asked, "Is pain real?" The doctor said, "Yes." The preacher then asked a series of questions. He asked, "Have you ever seen pain?" The doctor said, "No." The preacher asked, "Have you ever heard pain?" The doctor said, "No."

The preacher asked, "Have you ever smelled pain?" The doctor said, "No." The preacher asked, "Have you ever touched pain?" The doctor said, "No." The preacher asked, "Have you ever tasted pain?" The doctor said, "No." Finally, the preacher said, "That ought to tell you that pain ain't real." The doctor said, "Oh, no, pain is real." The old preacher asked, "How do you know that pain is real?" The doctor said, **"I know that pain is real because I can feel it."**

-The preacher said, "I'm glad you mentioned that because that's how I know that God is real. I know that God is real, for I can feel Him deep down inside of me."

17

The Reason We Preach the Death and the Resurrection of Jesus

My brother, the Reverend Dr. James C. Wade, Jr., pastor emeritus of the Zion Baptist Church of East Chicago, Indiana, said to me that a young man came to his house to talk to him. He said that the young man did not wait for him to get to his office.

When he invited the young man into his house, the young man said that he wanted to ask my brother a question. After my brother consented to hear the young man's question, the young man said, "Rev, why is it that every time you preachers preach, you always got' to say that Jesus died, was buried, and rose from the grave?"

My brother responded by saying, "Young man, I'm going to answer your question, but before I answer your question, I want to ask you some questions." My brother said, "Why is it that every time I see a baseball game, somebody is trying to cross home plate? Why is it that every time I see a basketball game, Michael Jordan is trying to get the rock in the rack? And why is it that every time I see a football game, they are trying to get the pigskin across the goal? And why is it that every time I see Tiger Woods, he's trying to get that white ball in the cup? And why is it that every time I see a hockey game, they are trying to get the puck in the net?"

The young man responded by saying, **"Oh, Rev, that's easy. The reason is that is how you win the game."** My brother said, "You wonder why we preachers have to say that Jesus died, was buried, and rose again? That's how our salvation was won."

-So, because that's how our salvation was won, don't think it to be redundant. Don't see yourself as a tautologist, or one who engages in unnecessary repetition. But keep on proclaiming the story that Jesus did die, was buried, but got up early Sunday morning.

18

Giving "All" in Worship

My brother James called me to give me two stories about his great-grandson Braylen. One Sunday afternoon, they had an afternoon service to attend. When it was time to get dressed, my brother said to Braylen, "Braylen, it's time to get dressed to go to church." Braylen, who was about five years old, said, "Paw Paw, I'm not going." Having been raised as we were, my brother did not take that response so well. So, he said again, "Braylen, it's time to get ready to go to church." Braylen again said, "Paw Paw, I'm not going." Now, my brother is about to really be upset. My brother said that he said to himself before he got mad, that he would ask Braylen why he was not going. So, he asked Braylen, "Why aren't you going?" Braylen responded by saying, **"Paw Paw, I'm not going because I don't have anything left. I gave it all at church this morning."**

> *-What a response to worship and praise! In a real sense, when you really worship and praise God according to the Bible, you really won't have anything left. I would like to recommend a book called, The Physical Side of Being Spiritual by Peter E. Gillquist.*

19

What to Do with Blessed, Healed, and Delivered Feet

Another incident between my brother James and his great-grandson Braylen:

My brother carried Braylen to get some shoes. When Braylen got the right shoes, he pointed his finger at his new shoes, and said, **"I'm going to have to teach you how to shout."**

And all of us who worship and praise the God of the Bible, ought to be like Braylen, **we need to teach our shoes how to shout.** When we look at Acts 3 and see the response of the lame man who was healed, he shows us what to do with blessed, healed, and delivered feet. The Bible says, "He went leaping . . . "

> *-And we as Christians do have blessed, delivered, and healed feet. Psalm 40:2 reads, "He brought me up also out of a horrible pit, out of the miry clay, and set my feet upon a rock, and established my goings."*

20

Powerlessness in the Church

There is a story that comes out of the Renaissance period: It is said that Thomas Aquinas visited the papal palace of Pope Innocent II. When Thomas Aquinas walked in, the Pontiff was counting a large sum of money. It is reported that when the Pope saw Thomas Aquinas, he said to him, "Look Thomas, the Church can no longer say to the world, 'Silver and gold have I none.'" Thomas Aquinas responded by saying, **"True, holy father, but neither can she now say, "Rise and walk."**

In these contemporary times, the Church is finding itself much like the nine disciples who could not heal the demon-possessed boy. We are experiencing a famine of power to deal with the ills of lame humanity.

> *-If we as the Church are going to rectify this power problem, there must be a concentrated return to the Bible and prayer, for that is where the power comes from, i.e., in association with the outpouring of the Holy Spirit.*

21

A Criteria Where Jesus Couldn't Fit

A young preacher candidated for a church that had no pastor. After preaching, he was told by the pulpit committee that he preached a wonderful sermon. He was told that although he preached a wonderful sermon, he did not fit their criteria-a pastor who was married, had a Ph.D., over 35 years old. Getting home in a spirit of disappointment, he wrote a letter, thanking them for the opportunity. Yet, he expressed sorrow over the fact that he did not meet their criteria. He stated that he was most sorry about the fact that their criteria were such that Jesus, the Head of the Church, could not fit. **He said, "Jesus did not have a Ph.D., was not married, and He died at the age of 33."**

> *-How sad that in churches' search for pastors, they have criteria that Jesus could not fit. Yes, a pastor ought to be prepared, but the Church ought to look for one mentioned in Jeremiah 3:15, which says, "I will give you pastors according to mine heart, which shall feed you with knowledge and understanding."*

22

God Wants Us as an Offering

A boy, whose parents were unbelievers, was invited by his neighborhood friend to go to church with him that particular Sunday. The boy seemed to have enjoyed everything that had transpired that Sunday. However, there was one thing that alarmed him. What alarmed him was the fact that the pastor called for the offering, and the boy had nothing to put in the offering basket.

That week, the alarmed boy thought about the fact that the pastor had called for the offering, and he had nothing to put in. All that week, he pondered about what he could put in the offering basket. Finally, it came to him what he could put in the offering basket. After having come to the decision of what he could put in the offering basket, he called his neighborhood friend and asked him if he could go to church with him. The neighborhood friend said, "Yes."

That Saturday night, the boy could not sleep because he wanted to go to church in order to put something in the offering basket. When he got to the church, the choir was singing. The boy said to himself, "I like the singing, but I will be glad when they get through singing and get to the offering because I have something to put in." Then, the pastor preached. The little boy said, "I like the preaching, but I will be glad when he is through and call for the offering because I have something to put in the offering."

Finally, the pastor said, "It's offering time." **The deacons brought the offering baskets, and without waiting for the ushers, the boy jumped up out of his seat, ran to the front, and jumped in the basket.**

The Apostle Paul says in Romans 12:1, "I beseech you therefore, brethren, by the mercies of God, that ye present your bodies a living sacrifice, holy, acceptable unto God, which is your reasonable service." Then, in II Corinthians 8:5a, it reads, "And this they did, not as we had hoped, but first gave their own selves to God."

-God does not want our possessions first. God wants us first. And the best thing that we can do, based upon the mercies of God, is to give ourselves to God.

23

Treat Everybody Right

There was a news story that a homeless man heard about a woman and her daughter who had been evicted. The homeless man went and found the lady and her daughter. When he found them, he took them and put them in a hotel. He gave the hotel manager more than $9,000.00, which he had collected standing on the corner. The lady, so astonished at what the homeless man had done, asked the homeless man why he was doing such a noble deed. The homeless man responded, **"The reason I am doing what I am doing is that when I stand on the corner every day, you were the only one who treated me like a human."**

-Be careful how you treat people because you never know who in life you will need. Og Mandino says, "Beginning today, treat everyone you meet as if they were to be dead by midnight. Extend to them all the care, kindness, and understanding you can muster, and do it with no thought of any reward." Jesus said in Matthew 7:12, "Therefore all things whatsoever ye would that men do to you: do ye even so to them." Then Paul writes in Galatians 6:7," Be not deceived; God is not mocked; for whatsoever a man soweth, that shall he also reap."

24

The Design of Preaching

One day, I was doing what I call, "sitting at my time of study." I was writing a sermon on Romans 1:16. I decided to print the term "preach" in pencil. I then turned my pencil upside down. I wanted to see if I could get a word within the word "preach." I began by crossing the "P," and I got the word "reach." I erased the "r," and I got the word "each." I then decided to erase the "e," and that phonetically pronounced the term "ache."

> *-It came to me that the design of "preaching" is to "reach each ache." That's why people should never stay home when there is something that aches them. For God, in His Word, has a Word that will reach their ache.*

25

Redemption Is Free

I read in "Biblical Illustrator" a story of an old lady whose daughter had a rare disease. Due to the disease, the daughter could only eat fresh fruit. One day, the old lady went searching for fresh fruit. Due to Winter, the old lady just knew fresh fruit would be quite expensive. The only place she saw fresh fruit was in the window of the king's royal greenhouse, inside the royal palace. While the old lady was looking at fresh fruit, a young lady went inside the greenhouse and began to put fresh fruit in a basket. After putting it in the basket, she went outside and handed the basket to the old lady. When she handed the old lady the basket, the old lady quickly said, "Ma'am, I can't afford to buy this basket of fresh fruit." The old lady tried to give the young lady a few coins she had. The young lady responded by saying, **"Ma'am this fruit is not for sale. What you should know is that I'm the princess, and my father is the King. And he is much too rich to sell, and you are much too poor to buy."**

-Is this not our redemption? God, our Father is too rich to sell, and because we are totally depraved, we are too poor to buy. Our redemption is free of charge.

26

Irritation Can Make You
Want to Quit

There was a news story about a man who walked from Los Angeles to New York. When the man finally arrived in New York, news reporters and cameramen were waiting for him. When he arrived, in an exhausted state, a news reporter asked him if, in his long journey, there was there a time he wanted to give up. The man said, "Oh, yes! There was a time when I wanted to give up." The news reporter asked, "Was it due to the desert heat?" The man said, "No." The reporter asked, "Was it due to the cold and the high mountains?" He said, "No." The reporter asked, "Was it because of the snow and rain?" The man said, "No." The reporter then said, **"What then was it that made you want to quit?" The man said, "It was the sand in my shoes."**

> *-How often is it that it is not the horrific and the catastrophic that makes you want to quit? But it is the annoying, irritable sand-like issues in your shoes.*

27

⟨⚭⟩

How to Handle the Demonic

A plane taxied down the runway, and just as the plane took flight, a flight attendant discovered a snake on board the plane. In a fearful panic, she radioed the pilot and said, "There's a snake on board this plane." Very calmly, the pilot asked, "What is he doing?" She said, "He is curled up, ready to strike." The pilot said, "Keep your eyes on him, and I will call you back."At that moment, the pilot immediately ascended. After ascending, he called back and asked what the snake was doing. The flight attendant said, "He's uncurling." The pilot ascended higher, called back, and asked what the snake was doing. The flight attendant said, "He is stretched straight out." Again, he ascended even higher and called back, and once again, asked what the snake was doing. The flight attendant said, "I'm glad to report that he has rolled over dead."

-There are some ascended heights that the demagogic snakes of this world cannot survive. That's the point that First Lady Michelle Obama made when she said at the Democratic National Convention, "When they go low, we go high."

28

Be Sure to Have the Right Key

Some years ago, I decided to take a vacation to Manhattan, New York. I made a reservation at the Hyatt Hotel on 43rd and Lexington. After checking in, I got my key and proceeded to check into my room. When I got to the door, I put my room key in the slot, and behold, it did not work. I tried several times to unlock the door, but to my chagrin and dismay, it would not open.

Having walked the long hall to my room when the key would not unlock the door, I thought to myself, "Now, I've got to walk back down the long hall, catch the elevator, and go back to the desk!" I was ticked off because the man at the desk had given me a key that did not work.

When I finally got to the desk, all ticked off, I said to the front desk person who checked me in, in a not-so-nice tone, "You gave me a key that don't work." The man said, "May I see your key?" I gave him my key, and he looked at it, and to my embarrassment, he said, "Sir, the reason this key won't unlock your door is that this key says, 'Doubletree,' and this is The Grand Hyatt."

What happened? The week before, I stayed in a Doubletree Hotel. What it boiled down to was that **I was trying to unlock this week's door with last week's key.**

Dealing with this Millennial Generation, are we not guilty of trying to unlock this generation's doors with the last generation's keys? Too many of us are missing them because we are irrelevant. The reason why we are irrelevant is that we have failed to be current and contemporary. We have failed to keep up.

> *-One writer has well said, "If you step outside of a swift rapid flowing water, by the time you step back in, you have not stepped into the same water." If we are to reach this generation, we must unlock the door with this week's key.*

29

Have What You Advertise

I was in the City of New Orleans in June, during the time of our National Baptist Congress. The headquarter hotel was The Sheraton on Canal Street. My dear friend and nephew Sam Gilbert II and I decided we wanted some Popeye's spicy fried chicken. Popeye's Fried Chicken was just across the street from our hotel. As you know, there is heat mixed with humidity during this time of the year. But we didn't mind going out into the heat because we had a real taste for Popeye's spicy fried chicken. When we got to Popeye's, there was a line of children and young people. We didn't mind that because it gave us some time to catch up. When we got to the counter to place our order, the lady had the temerity tell us that they had french fries, sodas, and fried pies; but no chicken. Based upon the fact that the sign did not say, "Popeye's french fries, sodas, and fried pies," but "Popeye's Chicken," **if they didn't have any chicken, that meant that they didn't have what they were advertising.**

> *-I'm convinced that in some instances, that's the way it is with some of our churches, i.e., we don't have what we are advertising.*

30

Remember to Say That "He Died"

In my early years of pastoring at Mt. Moriah Baptist Church in Los Angeles, one of the preachers of the church was an old man by the name of Reverend Smiley Mitchell. Reverend Smiley was never on time for worship. He was always late. Smiley always wore a beige raincoat that was always open. So, when he walked from the back of the church down the aisle, it would always swing behind him. When Reverend Smiley would walk, he had a cool walk because his left shoulder was always drooped. After making the long walk down the aisle, he would walk up to the pulpit and sit between some of our ministers. He would look at them as if they had lost their minds. After looking at them, he would say to them, "He died. Didn't He die? Amen! God Almighty!" What I didn't say at the outset was that Reverend Smiley Mitchell was senile. **But he was so gripped by the death of Jesus until even in senility, he didn't forget that Jesus did die.** It would seem to me that if old Smiley Mitchell didn't forget that He died, it would seem to me that those of us who are "clothed in our right minds" ought not to have a problem saying, "He did die. Amen! God Almighty!

-Old preachers taught that preaching is taking a text and bending a path to the Cross. But they also said, "Don't stop there. Take Jesus down from the Cross. Put Him in a borrowed grave." Then, remember to say, as the old Baptist preachers used to say, "Early, early, Sunday morning, He got up from the grave, and said, 'All power in Heaven and in Earth is in My hands!'"

31

God Can Get Beauty Out of the Ugly

From December 1997 through February 1998, there was a weather phenomenon that hit Southern California called, "El Nino." Scientists don't know what really triggers El Nino. What we do know is that there was a deluge amount of rain associated with it. For several months, there was a relentless string of storms that struck Los Angeles, causing much havoc and destruction. Roads and railroad tracks were washed away. Control channels overflowed, causing flooding. There were 17 known deaths. In total, there was a half-trillion dollars in damage in California during this El Nino cycle. On ABC (Channel 7 in Los Angeles) the field reporter Bob Banfield did a news story in conjunction with the El Nino phenomenon. He reported that **in the midst of all the destruction caused by El Nino, there were flowers blooming in the desert.**

-This affirms the fact that no matter how ugly and horrific a situation is, God, who is well able, can bring beauty out of the ugly and the horrific.

32

A Christian Departure to
Heaven

On June 8, 1924, a 38-year-old British schoolteacher named George Mallory, along with a 28-year-old Cambridge student named Andrew Irvine, set out to climb the tallest mountain. The mountain is Mount Everest. Mount Everest is 29,029 feet tall. It is reported that Mr. Mallory said that it was perfect weather for mountain climbing. When Mr. Mallory and Mr. Irvine were on their summit attempt, there was a mist that swallowed them. There was a teammate whose name was Noel Odell who was with them. Because Mallory and Irvine were swallowed by the mist and vanished, all that Mr. Odell could report was, *"LAST SEEN, REACHING FOR THE TOP."*

> *-And that's what could be said of Believers who God takes away from us, "LAST SEEN, REACHING FOR THE TOP."*

33

God's "With-Us-Ness" Presence

When our granddaughter Sydne' was small, we use to buy milk. On one side of the milk was printed the word for the day. One day, on the side of the milk was the word palindrome. "Palindrome" means, "a word, line, verse, number, or sentence that reads the same backward and forward." In reading the Bible, there is a verse that means the same forward and backward.

The latter part of Hebrews 13:5 reads, "**I will never leave thee, nor forsake thee.**" Reading it backward, it reads, "**Thee forsake nor, thee leave never will I.**"

> *-This further affirms the "With-Us-Ness" presence of God in the life of the Believer.*

34

Preaching Based On "I Know"

An old pastor, in the middle of his sermon, said to his parishioners, "The more I preach, the less I believe what I preach." His congregants looked at him with a look of utter shock. While they were in a state of shock, he then said, **"The reason that I am believing less, is because I'm knowing more."**

I can relate to this old pastor because I am a LEVEL THREE preacher-pastor. When I got saved, and when I started pastoring at the age of 20, all I could talk about was, "I heard." But then, I began to focus and study, and I moved from **LEVEL ONE**, the "I Heard" level, to **LEVEL TWO**, which is the "I Believe" level.

> *-But since I have been pastoring, I have been in the furnace of affliction, the den of trials and tribulation, and the school of hard knocks. And God has seen me through. So, I am not a fledging neophyte; I am no longer a beginner. And because I have graduated again, I'm not talking and preaching about what I heard or what I believe, but I'm at LEVEL THREE. Thus, I am preaching more about what "I Know."*

35

God Is About Shaping Us

A little boy made a boat and went to the lake to try it out. Upon trying it out, the boat got beyond his reach. Seeing the boy's dismay, his elder brother began throwing rocks at the boy's boat. The younger brother, not understanding the older brother's motive, tried to fight his brother to stop him so the brother would not destroy his boat. The elder brother, knowing his younger brother didn't understand what he was doing, lovingly wrapped his younger brother in his arms and turned him around. When the younger brother turned, he saw his boat coming back to shore. The older brother said to his younger brother, "You thought I was throwing "at" your boat. I was not throwing "at" your boat, I was throwing "beyond" your boat to create some ripples and waves in the water, to bring your boat back to the shore."

> -There are times God looks like He's throwing "at" us to destroy us. The fact is that God is not throwing "at" us to destroy us. No, God is not throwing "at" us to shatter us. He is throwing "beyond" us to create some ripples and waves in our water to shake us and bring us closer to Him so that He might shape us.

36

I Don't Live Where I Work

The story is told of a young woman who was hired as a live-in maid on a very rich estate. The young woman was to not only cook and clean, but she was also to be a nanny and help raise the children of wealthy parents. Eventually, the parents who hired her died, but by then, the children she raised were now grown and married. They remained in the mansion, and they had children who she raised. The children of the parents who hired her died, but she raised another generation of children. By then, she was no longer a young lady. She was then, an old woman. The second set of children she raised had a family meeting and decided to let this old woman, who they called, "Auntie," go.

After telling her that they had to let her go and find someone much younger, they asked her what she wanted them to do for her. She said, "Call me a cab." She went upstairs to her room and packed her few little things in a box. After coming downstairs, with tears lapping under her chin, she kissed everybody goodbye and got in the cab. The cab driver who she knew asked her where she wanted to go. She said, "Go to the third light, and turn left. Then, go to the second light, and turn right. Then, go to the first stop sign, and turn left."

When he made the left turn at the stop sign, he started going up a hill. When he got to the top of the hill, she said, "Pull over and stop." When he stopped, he looked out of his window to the right and saw a vacant lot. He said, "Auntie, why do you want me to stop by this vacant lot? She said, "You are looking in the wrong direction. Look to your left." When he looked to the left he saw a beautiful house with beautiful grass, trees, and flowers. The cab driver said, "Who lives here?" She said, "I do." The cab driver said, "I thought you lived back down there at the mansion. She said, "No. I just worked down there. This is what she said:

> *-But I knew the day was coming when I couldn't work anymore, I started making preparations. So, when it was time for me to move, I would have someplace to go."*

37

We Really Belong to God

Once, a little boy made himself a boat. After making the boat, he went down to the river to test it. Because of the current of the river, the boat got away from him. So, the boat he had made got lost. Sometime later, the boy was walking down the street and passed a pawn shop. In looking through the window of the pawnshop, he noticed there lay his boat. Excitedly, the boy ran into the pawnshop, reached upon the shelf and grabbed the boat that he made.

The owner of the pawnshop told the boy to put the boat back on the shelf. The boy said to the owner, "Sir, you don't understand, this boat is mine. I made it." The pawnshop owner said, "Son, if you want this boat, you will have to pay $2.50 first."

The boy ran home, got some bottles, and sold them. Then, after canvassing the neighborhood, he got a job cutting grass. Having earned enough money to buy his boat, he ran back to the pawnshop, placed the $2.50 on the counter, ran to the shelf, grabbed his boat, and clutched it to his chest. He then said to the boat, **"Boat, you are mine. You are really mine. In fact, you are mine twice. You are mine first because I made you. And now, you are mine twice because I bought you."**

-And that's God's Gospel, Good News, and message to every Believer. "You are mine twice," says the Lord. "You are mine first because, in Creation, I made you. But you are mine twice, because on Calvary, because of the death of my beloved Son Jesus, I bought you."

38

Jesus Is the Answer

The story is that there was a young productive man with a wife and three children. One day, the man was laid off from his job. Eventually, his unemployment checks ran out. When that happened, his house note was due, but he had no money. His car note was due, but he had no money. He needed food for his family, but he had no money. He said he wanted to do something productive in order to get some money to make ends meet. However, he said that he didn't want to resort to "the ungodly" to make ends meet.

So, he went to the Job Corp to see if he could get a job. However, there were no jobs available. He went to the employment office, but there were no jobs available. He went to the Social Security office, but there was no help available. He went to United Way and asked if they could help, but there was no help available. He went to the Salvation Army for clothes, but they were out of his children's clothes sizes. He then decided to go home and commit suicide. He figured that if he committed suicide, his family could get his insurance policy. Then, He said, "Before I take my life, let me see if I have covered all my options." He took some paper and this is what he wrote:

Job Corp-No job
Employment Office-No job
Social Security-No help
United Way-No help
Salvation Army-No Help

-*All of a sudden, God got in his eyes, and he saw, "J," for Job Corp; "E," for Employment Office; "S," for Social Security; "U," for United Way; and "S," for Salvation Army. He said, "I think I've found my answer - J.E.S.U.S. The letters "J.E.S.U.S." spell Jesus. Jesus is my answer. Jesus is my help. Jesus is my Hope!"*

39

Fathers Needed to Save Our Sons

My friend Freddie Haynes, my wife, and my children incited and literally goaded me to watch the movie, "The Lion King". I discovered as I watched the movie, "Lion King", that Scar was the low-down, jealous brother of the king. Scar was jealous of and had "hateration" for his brother Mufasa and his nephew Simba, who was heir to the throne. Scar hated on them and was jealous and low-down when he conspired with a herd of hyenas.

Lions and hyenas are each other's most common competitors because they consume the same prey. So, Scar the lion conspires with his enemies, the hyenas, to stampede in order to kill the heir-apparent Simba and King Mufasa. Scar set Simba up to be killed via a conspiracy. However, when King Mufasa gets word that his son Simba has been conspired against, and was in danger of being killed, Mufasa did not send Simba's mother to deliver him. He did not send some agencies or social services to deliver Simba. But when he knew that his son was in trouble, he went himself. **He did not send a substitute.**

He did not even send a surrogate to do what he was father enough to do. King Mufasa says, in essence, "If my son is to be delivered, I'm the one who will be responsible for his deliverance." The end result was that Mufasa's son was delivered, even though it cost Mufasa his life. Mufasa gave his life to save his son.

> *-As African-American fathers, we must take the position of the father of Mark 9:14-29 and King Mufasa. We must agree that if our boys are going to be saved from this covert conspiracy, we must be the agents and the catalysts for their deliverance. As men, we've got to think about something greater than sex. We must say, "If we were man enough to father them, we must be father enough to raise them."*

40

It's Time to Let Go

When I was in college, there was a newspaper article telling about a man who drowned in the ocean while rescuers were trying to save him. The rescuers reported why the man died. The report was that he would not let go of some heavy gold that he had tied around his waist. Rather than let the gold go, which is what rescuers were trying to get him to do, **he refused the call to let go, and he died in the very presence of the rescuers.**

> *-I'm here to tell us that we must let go of some of the stuff that has us weighed down. We are going to die mentally, emotionally, physically, and spiritually if we don't let some stuff of this world go. If we want to live, then we must let go of the world's stuff that has us weighted down, and could ultimately cause our demise.*

41

Arrogance Has No Place in the Pulpit

The story is reported that Dr. Charles H. Spurgeon invited a young seminary student who had just received his Ph.D. degree to preach one Sunday morning. The young seminarian invited all of his friends to hear him preach.

That Sunday, very proudly and arrogantly, with an uplifted head, the young man walked into the pulpit to preach. The young seminarian preached his sermon, but he was a miserable failure. Very dejectedly, with a hung-down head, he walked out of the pulpit.

When the worship was over, the young man walked into Dr. Spurgeon's office with a bowed head. Dr. Spurgeon said to the young seminarian, "Young man, I don't have the education that you have. However, I do know that **if you had walked into that pulpit like you walked down, then you could have walked down like you walked up."**

Arrogance and haughtiness do not belong in the pulpit. God uses preachers on an "in spite of" basis. In spite of our sins, iniquities, and frailty, God, in His Sovereign providence uses us anyhow. And the thanks that God ought to get is for preachers to have humble spirits. It does not matter how many persons we preach to; there ought to be within every preacher, a spirit of thankfulness and humility. *We should know that God chooses to use us, but God is never out of options.*

Remember, God always has options. Proverbs 6:16-17 tell us that God hates pride! Then, Proverbs 16:18 reads, "Pride goeth before destruction and a haughty spirit before a fall." Then, verse 19 says, "Better it is to be of a humble spirit with the lowly, than to divide the spoil with the proud."

> *-Let me reiterate the fact that there is no place for arrogance in the pulpit.*

42

How Many Times Has the Bible Been Through You?

E. K. Bailey said that one day, his father Dr. V. M. Bailey was in the barbershop getting a shave. While getting a shave, he was asked by a gentleman, "How many times have you been through the Bible?"

Dr. Bailey responded by saying:

> -"Sir, I'm not concerned about how many times I've been through the Bible. My real concern is how many times the Bible has been through me."

43

Prayer Works

One night, when all of the Wade children were small and Marsha was the baby, we visited relatives in eastern Oklahoma, where our father was born, and then, Tulsa, where his brother lived.

The night we were to leave to return to Omaha, Nebraska, our home, there was an awful rainstorm. Not knowing that the rain had flooded underpasses, we took to the highway. Without warning, we ran into a flooded underpass. The water was so deep that it killed the motor in our car. Daddy tried to restart the car so that we could back out. The car would not start. The longer we sat in that flooded underpass, the more the water came into our car. The water seeped into the trunk of our car and ruined the clothes in the trunk. As a small boy, **I remember Momma and Daddy engaged in strong prayer . . .**

-That night, I had the chance to see the power of prayer, because WITHOUT TURNING THE IGNITION, the car suddenly started, and Daddy was able to back up out of the flooded underpass. As a result, the seven of us were able to escape drowning.

44

The Greatest Thought

Dr. James S. Stewart, in describing the Swiss Theologian Dr. Karl Barth said, "This colossus of a Theologian is basically concerned about simple things." And the proof of Dr. James S. Stewart's description is illustrated in an incident described by Dr. James Montgomery Boice. Dr. Boice wrote, "Several years before his death, the Swiss Theologian, Karl Barth, came to the United States for a series of lectures. After a very impressive lecture, a student asked a typically American question. He said, "Dr. Barth, what is the greatest thought that has ever passed through your mind?" The aging professor paused for a long time as he obviously thought about his answer.

It is said that all of the seminary students were sitting on the edge of their seats waiting to hear some great theological systematic treatise, or some professional, deep, and complicated answer . . .

-Dr. Barth, raising his shaggy gray hair, looked at the student with the greatest simplicity, and said, "JESUS LOVES ME, THIS, I KNOW. FOR THE BIBLE TELLS ME SO."

45

The Christian's Tug of War

When I went through my bone marrow transplant experience, I was informed I would have to deal with GVH, the acrostic for Graft Versus Host. I was the host. My brother's marrow was the graft. Notice the middle word is "versus." The term versus means, "against." When "versus" is used, it is primarily referring to "opposition." What was inside of me before my transplant was slowly killing me. What was engrafted in me was to make me alive. So, what was inside of me had the audacity to fight against what was engrafted in me. **I think we Believers suffer from spiritual GVH.** There is guerilla warfare going on inside of us. There is a fight between our old demonic nature and the new nature of Christ in us. *-Paul even affirms this as he says in Romans 7:15-21 (KJV), "For that which I do, I allow not: for what I would, that do I not; but what I hate, that do I. If then I do that which I would not, I consent unto the law that it is good. Now then it is no more I that do it, but sin that dwelleth in me. For I know that in me (that is, in my flesh,) dwelleth no good thing: for to will is present with me; but how to perform that which is good I find not. For the good that I would I do not: but the evil which I would not, that I do. Now if I do that I would not, it is no more I that do it, but sin that dwelleth in me. I find then a law, that when I would do good, evil is present with me."*

46

Don't Be Ashamed of That Name

One evening, I was waiting to be picked up to go to preach in a revival service. For some reason, I left my television on, which I rarely do. The television was on mute. While my television was on mute, I noticed there were three beautiful black women on, and I could tell by their movements that they were singing. So, I turned my television sound up so that I could hear what they were singing. I saw where they were called, 'Destiny's Child." Their names were Kelly, Beyoncé, and Michelle. I listened as they sang, "Say my name, say my name. If you ain't runnin' game, say my name. Prove yourself to me, say my name."

> -When I had the time to really reflect, I could hear God saying, "If you love Me like you say you love Me, say My name. If this ain't no game, say My name. Prove yourself that you love Me by saying My name."

47

The Church Is the Way Home

Rev. J. Castina Jackson, the pastor of the Paradise Baptist Church of Tulsa, Oklahoma, told that one day, one of the young boys who was a member of his church got lost. Being lost, he became bewildered that he could not find his way home.

Finally, a policeman found him wandering aimlessly. When the policeman found him, the boy told the policeman that he was lost. The policeman asked him his name. He could not remember his name. The policeman asked him the name of his parents, but the boy being so bewildered could not remember their names. The policeman then asked, if there was anything that he could remember.

> -*The boy thought and thought, and finally said to the officer, "I'm a member of The Paradise Baptist Church. Rev. J. Castina Jackson is my pastor. IF YOU CAN GET ME TO THE CHURCH, I CAN FIND MY WAY BACK HOME."*

48

Delay Can Send You to Hell

The story in "Biblical Illustrator" magazine is that some imps were being dispatched by Satan to Earth to ruin men by persuading them not to turn to God. When he was to dispatch the first angel, Satan asked him what he would tell them. The first demon said, "I will tell men there is no Heaven." The Devil said, "No, don't tell them that because deep within them, something tells men there is a Heaven."

He then asked the second demon what he would tell the man. The second demon said, "I will tell them there is no Hell!" The Devil said, "Please don't tell them that because they are experiencing Hell on Earth."

He asked the third demon, what he would say to the man. The third demon said, **"I will tell them there is no hurry." The Devil replied, "Tell them that, and you will ruin them by the millions."**

Paul writes in II Corinthians 6:2 these words, "For He saith, I have heard thee in a time accepted, and in the day of salvation have I succored thee: behold, now is the day of salvation."

There is a Proverb that says, "Procrastination is the thief of time." **But I have found that procrastination is the thief of souls.**

Benjamin Franklin said, "You may delay, but time will not, and lost time is never found again."

Edward Young says, "Procrastination usually results in sorrowful regret."

Psalm 95:7 and 8a reads, "Today if you will hear his voice, harden not your heart."

Isaiah 55:6 states, "Seek you the Lord while He may be found, call ye upon Him while He is near."

Today is the only time that men know they have. For tomorrow is not promised.

K. Lyons put it like this, "Yesterday is a canceled check; tomorrow is a promissory note; today is the only cash you have; so spend it wisely."

> *-Today is decision time; not tomorrow.*

49

Lessons on the Church Being
Incendiary

When my siblings and I were children, our father taught us great lessons. The first lesson was found on 24th and Seward, in Omaha, Nebraska.

On 24th and Seward was an ice house. Our father showed us that people come to an ice house, get ice, and leave. **His lesson teaches us that no one hangs out at an ice house.**

Lesson two came one night when Reverend Marion, who lived on 27th Street between Decatur and Franklin (just around the corner from where we lived), lived in a house that caught on fire. After the firemen had doused the fire and had returned back to the fire station, Daddy pointed out lesson two. Even though the fire was out, people were still standing around where the fire was. **Our father told us that people hang around where there is a fire.**

Daddy said, "If we turn the church into an ice-house, people will not hang around. But let the church catch fire, and people will come to where there is a fire.

I remember hearing that a church was on fire in a small community. By the time the firemen arrived, the fire had been put out. The person who put the fire out was a man who never went to church. The pastor found out who put the fire out, and went to the man. He said to the man, "We have tried to get you to church for a number of years, and you refused us. Now, here you are at the church. The pastor asked, "Why?" The man said, "I'm here because this is the first time that I've seen this church on fire."

> -In Acts 2, when the church was on fire, the Bible says that a multitude came. If the church breaks out on fire, under the power of the Holy Ghost, someone will come.

50

Good News About John 3:16

My brother James told me of a little boy who got lost. The boys had been lost for some time. Finally, he was encountered by a policeman. The boy was wet, smelly, cold, dirty, tired, and hungry. The policeman gave him directions to a church. The policeman said to the boy, "You will know that it's the right church because, on the top of the church, it says, "John 3:16."

When the boy walked into the church, the pastor was preaching about John 3:16. While in the service, a man spotted this boy, and after talking with the boy, he carried the boy home with him. When the man got into the home, it was nice and warm. As the boy was warming up, he said to himself, "I sure wish I knew what John 3:16 says."

Next, the man said, "Go upstairs and take a bath, and there will be some clean clothes for you." After taking the bath and putting on the clean clothes, he pondered to himself, "I wish I knew what John 3:16 says."

The boy then heard the man calling him down to eat. As he sat at the table, and while feeding himself, the little boy thought silently, "I wish I knew what John 3:16 says."

Finally, the man said, "It's time to go to bed," and he showed him his bed. After getting under the cover, the boy said, "I wish I knew what John 3:16 says."

As the boy recaptured what happened to him that day, he began to say to himself, **"I don't know what John 3:16 says, but what I do know is that John 3:16 will take in a lost boy, it will warm a cold boy, it will clean a dirty boy, it will clothe a naked boy, it will feed a hungry boy, and it will rest a tired boy."**

-The fact of the matter is that the God of John 3:16 is Yahweh-Jireh. And the nomenclature Yahweh has a dual meaning. One is, "The God who sees," and the other is, "The Lord will provide." The God of John 3:16 sees our needs and then provides for our needs. Philippians 3:19 says, "But my God shall supply all your needs according to His riches in glory." God's vision is inextricably tied to God's provision.

51

God's Divine Weeble

There is an American company that produces educational toys and games for children. The name of the company is Playskool. It is head-quartered in Pawtucket, Rhode Island. In 1971, Playskool came out with a roly-poly toy called, "Weeble." Weeble is a toy that rights itself when pushed over. Weeble had a very popular catchphrase. That catchphrase was, "Weebles wobble, but they don't fall down."

The reason Weebles wobble, but they don't fall down is because there is a weight located at the bottom center that causes it to be lifted off the ground. Once released, gravitational force brings the Weeble back into an upright position. In essence, **the reason Weebles wobble, but they don't fall down, is because of the "stuff inside."**

We wonder why we as Christians can face great catastrophic cataclysms and they reel and rock our world, but we don't fall apart. God has given us some Divine Weeble. We got some stuff on the inside that helps us to stand up straight, even though the winds blow.

What is the stuff on the inside that keeps us from falling in the midst of the horrendous winds that blow?

We have the abiding presence of Jesus.

We have the indwelling of the Holy Spirit.

We have the peace that passes all understanding.

We have mountain-moving faith.

We have lion-like tenacious courage.

We have perfect love that casts out fear.

We have unspeakable joy.

We have immutable Divine promises.

We have the fruit of the Spirit.

We have the mind of Christ.

We have the Word and power of God.

-Sister Lucie Campbell, the Gospel singer who was so dedicated to Gospel music that she turned down $50.00 to play the Memphis blues, saw a blind man who played church songs on the street. She wrote the song lyrics, "Something within me, that holdeth the reigns. Something within me, that banishes pain. Something within me, I cannot explain. All that I know, there is something within."

5²

What You Need Is in
the Word

A young man, somewhat profligate and prodigal, decided to leave home. About to leave, his mother gave him a Bible in a box. She said, "Son, if you ever get in need, read your Bible." He promised he would. One day, having spent all, in desperate need, he called his mother and told her he was broke and in a crisis to pay rent. She asked, "Do you remember what I told you when you left home?" He said, "Yes. If I ever get in need, read my Bible." She said, "Did you do it?" He said, "Yes, Mama." She said, "No, you didn't." He said, "Yes, I did." She said again, "No, you didn't. The reason I know is that you're calling me. If you read the Bible like I told you, you wouldn't be in need." She said, "Go get the Bible out of the box." When he got the Bible, she told him the verses to find. In every scripture, she told him to find, there was a $100 bill.

> *-It is an axiomatic fact that whatever you need is in the Word of God. "Axiomatic" means, "A truth so obvious that it doesn't need any proof."*

53

A Reason to Shout In
Worship

There was a woman who shouted every Sunday. In fact, she would shout so hard until the ushers had to take her out in order to revive her. One day, members of the "No Shout Every Sunday Committee" had a group discussion about her. They said they wanted to have a meeting with her to find out what all the shouting was about. They said, "We got ligion' just like she got ligion', and we don't shout every Sunday. You know 'REB' don't preach that good every Sunday. But no matter what, she got to shout every Sunday. And the choir don't sing that well every Sunday. But no matter what, she got to shout, and the ushers got to take her out. So we need to meet her to find out what she's shouting about." The committee just knew she had a hidden agenda. So, they confronted her and asked for a meeting. When they met with her, they said to her, "We wanted to meet with you because we need to know what this shouting every Sunday is about. We know that we got ligion' just like you got ligion'. We shout every now and then, but not every Sunday. We know that 'REB' don't preach that well every Sunday. And the choir don't sing that well every Sunday. So, what we want to know is, why is it that you have to shout every Sunday?"

The lady said, "I'm glad you asked because I really want you to know why I shout every Sunday. The reason that I shout every Sunday is that when I come to church, I come with one thought in my mind, and that is, I come looking to see Jesus. On the Sunday's that the choir sings good, and the pastor preaches good, I look directly at them, see Jesus, and I shout. On Sundays, the choir does not sing well, and the pastor does not preach well, I look around them, I see Jesus, and I shout."

My brother James says that there are two times that you ought to praise the Lord and shout. He said, "When you feel like it, and when you don't feel like it." Psalm 5:11 reads, "But let all those that put their trust in thee rejoice; let them ever shout for joy because thou defendest them." In Psalm 32:11 we read, "Be glad in the Lord and rejoice, ye righteous: and shout for joy, all ye that are upright in heart." And then in Psalm 47:1, it is written, "O clap your hands, all ye people; shout unto God with the voice of triumph." In the Old Testament, we read constantly about Israel shouting. They shouted before Calvary and the resurrection. And it seems to me that all of us who are "Post-Calvary" and the resurrection of Jesus have a greater reason than the Old Testament servants. Our greater reason is that Jesus did die, and was buried, but early Sunday, He got up with all power in His hands.

> *-I remember hearing these words: "When you think, you thank. When you remember, you rejoice. When you ponder, you praise. When you look back, you leap up." Then the song says, "When I think of the goodness of Jesus, and all He's done for me, my soul cries out, Hallelujah!" Then the praise song says, "When I think of His goodness and what He's done for me. When I think of His goodness, how He set me free. When I think of His goodness, and what He's done for me. When I think of His goodness, how He died on Calvary. I just dance, dance, dance, all night."*

54

⟨⟩∞⟨⟩

When God Answers Prayer, You Ought to Say, "Thank You"

There was a lady who went to church every Sunday with her grand-daughter. All through the service, she would shout out four words. Those four words were, "Oh, God, thank You!" Some members of the church eventually got annoyed with this woman's four words, "Oh, God, thank You!" So, they asked if they could come by where she lived. Excitedly, thinking the members wanted to fellowship with her, the old grandmother said, "Sure."

When the members came into her home in the projects, they said to the old lady, "The reason why we have come is that we have grown tired of your loud four words in church. We want to know why you keep saying those four words loud in the church?"

The old lady responded by saying, "As you can see, me and my grand-baby live in the projects, all alone, and this is a bad neighborhood. This area is filled with a lot of gangs, and at night, there is always a lot of shooting. When I hear the shooting, I grab my grandbaby, and we hit the floor and hide under the bed. When we hit the floor, I cover her up, and then I pray, 'Oh, God.' When we wake up in the morning, and I see that we are still alive and have not been harmed, I say, 'Thank you!' My grandbaby goes to a rough school. So, I take her to catch the bus. When she catches the bus, I wait for her to get off the bus. And when she gets off of the bus, I say 'Oh, God,' and when I see that she's alright, I say, 'Thank you.'"

When I was a boy, our forefathers had a lot of "thank" in their prayers. Reminisce with me for a moment, and hear the prayers of the Saints of old.

> -"Our Heavenly Father, it is your weak and humble servant coming before you, knee bent and body bowed, coming before you as an empty pitcher before a full fountain; to give you some sincere and humble thanks. Lord, I want to thank you for last night's lying down and this morning's early rising. Lord, I thank you that my bed was not my cooling board, and the cover that I covered with was not my winding sheet, and the four walls of my room were not the four walls of my grave. And when I woke up this morning, I didn't wake up in The Judgment. My eyes beheld a brand-new day, one that I had never seen before and will never see again. Lord, I thank you that the blood is still running warm in my veins, and I am clothed in my right mind. Lord, I thank you that you have allowed my golden moments to roll on a little while longer." Like our forefathers, we have so much to thank God for. "Thank you!"

55

Has God Really Turned His Back on You?

A young lady was having a lot of bad situations in her life. The young lady went to a mature Christian woman and began to complain to the mature woman about the bad circumstances and troubles that were occurring in her life. The young lady concluded her complaint by saying, "God has turned His back on me."

-After pondering the young lady's complaint and conclusion for a moment, the mature Christian woman, knowing that the young lady was not praying, reading her Bible, and had ceased going to worship, responded by saying, "How can God turn His back on you, when you are never in His presence?"

56

Young People, Take the
Weapon of the Word

There was an old western movie where a young man graduated from dental school. To his mother's shock, surprise, and dismay, the son told his mother he wanted to go west because there were just too many dentists in the East. He said, "In the West, you will find no real scientific study." So, he wanted to go to fertile ground. When the son was ready to head west on the train, his mother went with him to the train station to see him off. Just as her son was about to board the train, to his surprise, his mother reached in her pocket and pulled out a Colt 45. Knowing the dangers of the West, the mother said to her son as she gave him the Colt 45, **"Son, as you go, you might need it."**

-As I think about it: When our children get ready to head out into a dangerous world, we as parents, know the evils and the demonic in this world, like this mother, we ought to give them a weapon. And that weapon is the Bible that they are going to need.

57

Let God Do What He Do

There was a lady who complained about needing help to clean her house because she was unable to do so. After hearing the complaint of his wife, the husband went and found an excellent housekeeper. The housekeeper was to start the coming Monday.

The Sunday afternoon prior to the day the housekeeper was to start, the husband noticed that his wife was quite busy doing something. The husband, having watched his wife frantically doing some things, said, "Honey what are you doing?" The wife said, "I'm cleaning up. I don't want the housekeeper to think that we are dirty." The husband said, "Honey, you admitted to me that this task was too big for you, and you were unable to do it. **So, since you were unable, and this task is too big for you, and since we have found someone who is able, let's just let the one who is qualified and able do what she is able to do.**"

How often do we hear people say that before they come to the church, they must get themselves right? However, there are some things that those who make such a resolve do not know.

First of all, they do not know that you cannot straighten out a crooked stick. Then, they don't know that from a spiritual standpoint, there is no such thing as self-liberation. Thirdly, they don't seem to discern the fact that the church is designed for the spiritually impaired. And finally, they don't know that God has cathartic and metamorphic power.

The term "cathartic" means "cleansing and purifying." And the term "metamorphic" means "change of form." Therefore, men do not need to try self-cleansing, but they need to come to the place where God can cleanse, purify, and change them.

> -The Roman African Christian Theologian and Philosopher, Saint Augustine of Hippo, said, "The Church is a hospital for Sinners, not a museum for Saints." So, let God do' what He do'.

58

My Best Days Are Yet to Come

There was a bright girl who was about 15 years old who became gravely ill. She was completely paralyzed on one side and nearly blind. The young girl could hardly see, but she could hear.

As she lay in her bed in the hospital, she heard the doctor talking to her parents. The doctor then said to her parents, "She has seen her best days . . . Poor child!"

-The girl who was a Believer in Jesus heard what the doctor said. The girl quickly replied after hearing the prognosis of the doctor. She said, "No doctor. My best days are yet to come; when I shall see my King in His beauty."

59

Staying Low Behind Our Shepherd

Once, I was watching Monday Night Football, and there was a running back who the opposition was trying its best to tackle. They were unable to tackle the guy because they, seemingly, "could not find him." Seemingly, the reason they "could not find him" was because of the fact that **he stayed low behind the big man in front of him.**

> *-If we as Believers are to avoid the assaults and attacks of our enemies–the Devil, the world, and the flesh, we must stay low behind the Omnipresent Shepherd who leads us.*

60

When You Need Him, Call Him

In 1963, I confessed my call to preach. On September 9, 1963, I preached what the old preachers called, "my trial sermon." The following day, my father drove me to Dallas, Texas, to enroll in Bishop College. Showing love and watching me adapt and adjust to leaving and being gone from home for the first time, Daddy stayed with me for several days.

Finally, my father told me that he had to return home so he could be in church that coming Sunday. However, before he departed, he said to me, "If you need me, call me."

One day, I was going through something, and I remembered Daddy saying to me, "If you need me, call me." I did not have any money to use the pay telephone. So, I borrowed a dime from a classmate. I put the dime in the pay telephone and made a collect call. Because there was no such thing then as "call waiting," the line was busy. I waited a while and made the same call. Once again, the line was busy. Finally, I made another call. This time, my mother answered the phone and accepted the charges.

After speaking to my mother, I asked for my father. My mother responded by saying, "Your daddy left for a revival this morning. He's on the train, but when he calls, I will have him call you."

Well, my father said, "If you need me, call me." I needed my father, and to try to get him, I had to borrow a dime, and dial the payphone. The line was busy, and my father was unavailable.

> *-But it came to me that I have another Father. I don't have to borrow a dime. I don't have to use a pay telephone. His line is never busy, and He's never unavailable. I can call Him day or night, and He even inclines or hears my faintest cry. The word "incline" means, "to lean forward and bow down to catch a sound that's too faint to be heard."*

61

Stand on the Word

There was a little boy playing in the basement of his house. While playing downstairs, a fire broke out upstairs. Because of the placement of the fire, the fire blocked the way to the basement. So, the mother ran outside and kicked the small window of the basement out. She leaned her head in the window and said to the boy, "Come out." The little boy said, "Momma, I'm not tall enough." The mother said, "Go and get that chair, and stand on it." He did that, but said, "I'm still not tall enough." The mother said, "Look and see if you see anything you can put on the chair, and come out." He saw an encyclopedia. He did that. He said, "I'm still not tall enough. She said, "Do you see anything else?" He said, "Yes, I see a dictionary." She said, "try that," and he did. He said, "I'm still not tall enough. The mother said, "Do you see something else?" He said, "Yes, Momma, I see a Bible." She said, "Go and get that Bible." He got the Bible. **When he stood on the Bible, he was tall enough to get out.**

-He was saved from perishing in the fire because he stood on the Word of God. If we are going to get out of the muddy mess we have made, then we must stand on the Word.

62

On the Reverend's Wall

The story is told that there was a couple who was on the brink of divorce. They called and made an emergency appointment with their pastor. When they went in to see the pastor, just before he asked them to sit down, they gazed at something on his wall, and said to him, "Never mind, pastor, we are alright now."

Later, they were discussing what happened in the pastor's office that reconciled their marriage. They said, "We read something on the Reverend's wall that handled our condition."

> *-They were asked, "What was it?" They said, "It was only two words." Somebody said, "What were those two words that were so powerful?" And they said, "The two words were, "GOD WILL!"*

63

Saved by the Blood

On May 24, 2022, an 18-year-old gunman, Salvador Rolando Ramos, shot and critically wounded his grandmother. After having critically wounding her, he went to The Robb Elementary School and went on a shooting rampage. He killed 19 elementary students, two teachers, and wounded 17 others.

In the aftermath of that devastating rampage, an 11-year-old surviving student named Mia Carrillo testified to a U.S. House Committee, via video, that she survived and did not die because she covered herself in the blood of her friend.

-I John 15:13 reads, "Greater love has no man than this, that a man lay down His life for His friend." The reason why we should have died and didn't is that we are covered with the blood of our FRIEND, JESUS.

Increase Your Vocabulary

When I was in Bishop College, my major professor, Dr. Richard Rollins, who we affectionately called, "Dean" would give us our syllabus. In the syllabus, he would include a list of vocabulary words to increase our vocabulary. So, even though this book is about illustrations, I want to do like Dean Rollins and include some vocabulary words. These are some words that I have encountered in my reading. And, hopefully, it will increase the vocabulary of those who read this book.

VOCABULARY

1. Abstemious - not self-indulgent, restraint in eating and drinking
2. Ad hominem - appealing to one's prejudice, emotions, or special interest rather than to one's intellect or reason
3. Adjudicate - to hear and decide a case and the decision is binding
4. Adroitness - clever in using the hands or mind
5. Adumbrate - to disclose partially
6. Aficionado - an ardent supporter, devotee, or fan
7. Agoraphobia - fear of going outside
8. Alacrity - cheerful readiness or promptness
9. Anacoluthic - a shift in an unfinished sentence
10. Anthropopathic - ascribing human feelings to God
11. Asomatus - incorporeal, having no material body disembodied
12. Attenuate - to reduce the effect or value of or to weaken the potency of

13. Autoschediasm - something that is improvised or extemporized
14. Axiom - a statement or proposition that is regarded as being an established, self-evident truth
15. Cathartic - bringing about purification or renewal
16. Celerity - rapidity of motion or action
17. Circumlocution - the use of an unnecessary number of words to express an idea
18. Cognoscenti - persons who have superior skills in a certain field
19. Consanguinity - of the same blood, or blood relation, common ancestor
20. Conundrum - a puzzle or riddle
21. Cornucopia - an abundant supply
22. Culpable - guilty or blameworthy
23. Dimorphic - capable of existing in two forms
24. Dirigible designed or capable of being directed, controlled, or steered
25. Dystopian - a society characterized by misery, oppression, disease, and overcrowding
26. Egregious - remorsefully flagrant
27. Emollient - having the power of softening or relaxing
28. Enigma - a person or thing that is mysterious, puzzling, or difficult to understand
29. Eremophobia - fear of being alone
30. Ergophobia - extreme fear of work
31. Eristica - a person who engages in controversy
32. Esoteric - intended to be understood by only a small number of people
33. Eudemonia - happiness or well-being
34. Euphoria - a state of intense happiness, excitement, a feeling of well-being
35. Ex Nihilo - out of nothing
36. Exacerbate - to become increasingly bitter, violent, or unpleasant
37. Exiguous - scanty, meager, or small

38. Extirpate - to pull up something by the root, to remove, or destroy totally
39. Fastidious - excessively critical or demanding
40. Faux Pas - a social blunder
41. Fugacious - fleeting or transitory
42. Gasconade - to boast or brag
43. Hubris - arrogant
44. Iconoclastic - characterized by an attack on cherished beliefs
45. Immolate - kill
46. Indubitable - unquestionable, undoubtable, and indisputable
47. Ineffable - incapable of being expressed or described in words
48. Insouciant - lack of concern or indifferent
49. Inveterate - habitual
50. Irrefragable- impossible to refute
51. Je ne sais Quoi - something that cannot be adequately described
52. Jejune - empty, barren, dry, uninteresting
53. Laconism - brevity or concise
54. Mnemonic - a technique of improving memory, or intended to assist memory
55. Modus vivendi - mode of living, a way of life, one that bypasses difficulty
56. Nefarious - wicked or criminal
57. Nostalgia - a wistful or excessive sentimental yearning for return to or of some past period; a state of being homesick
58. Obsequious - obedient to an excessive servile degree
59. Obstreperous - unruly, noisy, difficult to control, disorderly, undisciplined
60. Onerous - burdensome or oppressive
61. Onomatopoetic - a word that sounds and resembles its meaning like "Bam"
62. Opulent - wealthy or abundantly rich
63. Paragonist - a perfectionist
64. Pejorative - to make or become worse

65. Perspicacious - quick mental discernment
66. Plausible - an argument or statement that seems reasonable or believable
67. Polemic - warlike, hostile, a controversial argument
68. Proliferate - increase rapidly in numbers or multiply
69. Propinquity- the state of being close or in proximity
70. Prurient - characterized by lascivious, lewd, unwholesome, licentious, appealing to sexual

THOUGHTS

1. Puissant - powerful or able
2. Pusillanimous - lacking courage or cowardly
3. Quid pro quo - something for something; a favor for a favor
4. Quiddity - the inherent nature or essence of someone or something social situations
5. Savoir-faire - to act or speak appropriately in
6. Senectitude - the final stage of the normal life span
7. Senescence - to grow old
8. Serendipitous - finding valuable things not sought for
9. Sesquipedalian - having many syllables or characterized by using long words
10. Simulacrum - an image or representation of someone or something
11. Sine-Qua Non - something absolutely indispensable
12. Solipsistic- when self is the only existing thing extreme egocentrism
13. Soporific - induce drowsiness or sleep
14. Spurious - false, fake, illegitimate, not real, bogus, counterfeit
15. Squalor - filth, and misery
16. Sui Generis - one of a kind, or in a class by itself
17. Supercilious - arrogant, haughty, superior, condescending
18. Surreptitious - clandestine or secretive

19. Sursum Corda - lift up your hearts
20. Tatterdemalion - ragged or disreputable in appearance; or being in a decayed stated; dilapidated or unkempt
21. Tenebrific - producing darkness
22. Terse succinct, concise, very brief
23. Tour de force - a feat of strength or an achievement that has been accomplished with great skill
24. Ubiquitous - existing or being everywhere, especially at the same time
25. Urbanity - refined courtesy or politeness
26. Verba - the exact words
27. Virtuoso - one with great technical skill in fire arts
28. Visceral - relating to deep inward feelings rather than to the intellect... a visceral feeling is intuitive
29. Vituperative - characterized by verbal abuse marked by harsh abusive criticism

CPSIA information can be obtained
at www.ICGtesting.com
Printed in the USA
BVHW052341130123
656259BV00020B/1115/J

9 781087 921044